LUNATIC SPEAKS

Caroline Hagood

FutureCycle Press

Mineral Bluff, Georgia

Published by FutureCycle Press
Mineral Bluff, Georgia, USA

ISBN 978-0-9839985-8-7

For Adriel, who loves the lunacy

Contents

Rewriting Red

Red is that place beneath my skin that knows
what I really am, the anger I stuffed in a shoebox
under my bed, the tension in the air right before
a bar fight, the aftermath of the longest wavelengths
of light, the color of the people we flayed
to make our new world, the shared hallucination
of human history,

the shade of the stop sign, Mars' iron oxide,
Devon cattle, the rouged faces of alpha mandrills,
the tails of retreating astronomical matter,
African mourning, Chinese wedding dresses,
Mao Zedong, that *red sun in the hearts*
of the people, and broken blood vessels,

the raw hamburger meat I used to sneak,
shake salt on, imagine to be what men tasted like,
lust-dusted, taken into the shadows of my body,
never to be seen again, and certain kinds
of coral, Anthozoa of Cridaria, colonies
of secreted calcium carbonate,

overcooked lobsters, the Cincinnati Red Stockings,
Republicans, and those flowers in my mother's book
that always reminded me of dog erections, waxy
with just the tip of something angry peeking out—
Anthuriums, she called them, but I could never bring myself
    to say the name—
and the eye where it has been entered by foreign matter.

The only way to rewrite red is to take it apart:
strip back the casing of the monster of history,
reduce it once again to its smallest pieces,
and then speak to them. Do not turn away
when the shucked mess gapes at you,
asks for its skin back. Speak.

1.

The Voyage In

The doctor will make you do it,
say you should know what you have
down there. Sleepless, you will pad

into the night bathroom, take a mirror
to that other nocturnal thing,
separate and haunting

in ways unspeakable.
Crouching on shaking legs,
you will survey glistening planes,

then stop, begin again.
What you see won't share
the grammar of beauty,

but it will be more provocative
than the smell of the city breathing;
not opera, but the tingling holler

of a storm; not light scatter,
but floodlight that goes on forever,
heaving, beating, breathing—

and you will be mesmerized,
so hopelessly in love,
you'll half expect it to speak.

Becoming a Woman

No, that first bloody swish
followed by a frantic trip
to the store for tampons

and mom's bashful explanation
of how to insert them
is not when you became a woman.

It wasn't even when you couldn't wait
to feel the salt-soft of someone else's mouth.
It was when you saw yourself

in a steam-cleared mirror and knew
you had a bit of danger in you.
Perhaps it seeped in while you watched your father

apply cream to battle his face hairs
that fell every morning to the white porcelain
like clear-cut trees. It wasn't only boys

who wanted a little shaver all their own
to understand their fathers through the removal
of stubborn pieces of themselves they didn't yet have,

to conquer rugged skin terrain like bathroom cowboys,
to later be able to plant and fell the trees of the world,
leaving behind only so much stubble.

Gender Studies

There's a little girl inside
who uses my mouth as a peephole,
cleans out my dollhouse sink with a sponge.

She thinks she might be me
but can't remember. She wishes
to be the kind of creature the world can't touch.

She knows she is not a man
but carries the stains of manhood—the stress
of weaponry, the sound of jackhammers,

the call to wear shirts with buttons,
to cultivate moustaches,
to get food stuck in beards.

Who is she if not a man?
She doesn't know, but she sketches
pre-language possibilities on her thighs,

walks daily past men who call out dirties to her.
She knows that underneath their lust
they struggle to find a name

for the namelessness in women.
She wants to discover the secret
language of equivalence,

beyond the turns and pivots
of definition, to strike down the difference
between things with a sword.

What Lolita Wishes She Could Say

There she is,
a young snow girl,
a slow see-thing in pain.

She remembers when blood fell
on her skin like undigested snow,
the last laugh of old Jack Frost.

As she sees it, people can be separated
into starers into the distance
and those who think it better left unseen.

But she knows the sights will continue
to fall down upon the eyes and non-eyes alike,
regardless, a planet of the periphery

orbiting always in the side mind
seen finally when the third eyelid rises.
Speaking of seeing, she wants to tell him

about the broken slants of light
where her inner barn was kicked in
by the horses.

She wants to tell him of the hay walls
she built in her mind
to hide the disfigurement.

Her past stalks her
like strained things seen
from the back of moving cars.

Her mind is a series of roadside
lights seen squintingly
until strangely luminescent.

She has a garbage man's knack
for making the rubbish of her life
into a chapel that is positively Sistine.

She dreams of hurricanes
and knows home to be
the broken in her.

Orphan in Love

She has mastered the art
of being unknown, of hiding
pleasure-shaken shoulders,

the soft side of the tongue,
and how she longs to press it,
peel it, hear it speak her name.

The animal of lushness
creeps unseen through her body.
She has a lover made of grass,

of the sound of lights falling on night fields.
She says there was a secret funeral for the imagination,
but the world just slept on through.

Every night she tears at the empty button on her belly
that once bound her to her mother,
before she turned her bones and left her baby.

She survived by seeing
how gorgeous raindrops are
on recently mown lawn,

that eyeless land uncovered,
still aglow with the science
that has been the noise in her.

2.

Andy Warhol with a Ukulele

They call me the Gremlin Girl,
a red tomato of a lass, so happy
spilling honey on the bees.

Even after being colonized,
cross-stitched into patterns,
and shot out of cannons,

I remain alabaster and seaweed,
porcelain and frog skin,
apple pie and Whore of Babylon.

I am pine tree, nutmeg, and a quick fix,
the most ladylike crow's foot
you've ever seen. I can spot myself

in slow motion entering
my own body, backstroking
through organs and blubber and miles of nerves.

Inside there is a little Blue Jay
building miniature cities and Andy Warhol
with a ukulele

fumbling along in skin borrowed
from a traveling salesman,
scars on the whitest parts of him.

Andy tells me *there's nothing of the butterfly in you,*
none of that magnificent poison—
but don't worry girl-child,

I'll hide you in the belly of a whale,
coat your face, body,
and fragmented heart in fish fat.

All you are is priceless—
you're the insurmountable, the part of the meat
people pay extra for.

My Inner David Lynch Movie

My thoughts are the things dogs dream about
when they whimper in their sleep.

Even my diary is scared of me, irked by my compulsion
to empty this warped head on paper, capture its rebel memories

in the jaws of endless yawning parentheses.
I was 11 and thought myself all-seeing;

staring at my leg tops shimmering in bubble bath,
I became convinced that these soaped-up limbs

were someone else's, that a mad Lynchian midget
had cleaved right around the knees and then left them,

severed and floating, in my soapy water.
Years later, the same boyfriend who told me I cried in my sleep

had a different theory about my legs. He swore that,
when crossed, they looked like folded bird wings.

He imagined them exhausted from aerial sojourns,
flying trapezes following the mad law of motion,

but even he had no idea how far out I could spiral, like tonight,
at that hour when to call it mental illness would be too easy—

when I call friends up to ask them if I'm still alive,
stiffened with over-thought, ready to faint or levitate,

convinced that the thing clinging
to my bathroom mirror is a tiny dragon wing,

that if I eat it my poetry book will be published.
Maybe I turned out this way because my mother says things like

Go put a button on your cheek and hang a piano from it
or because I once ate Cheetos on the toilet while listening to
    heavy metal.

I know it's getting grim when I start deconstructing cheddar
    things
and googling "how to tell if I'm dead," so I've tried to make
    my delirium

into something I could serve at a dinner party.
Still, it reeks of loneliness and nobody wants it.

All I can do is take night's madness and put it in a blender,
let the choppers go at it, silver with rage and other panics,

until it rains the mind slop I drain into Tupperware daily:
baby doll heads flickering in the ether, wind tunnels,

smashed piggybanks, pigeon juice and ceiling wax,
tufts of rat fur and Chinese finger traps, the last unicorn

carved up and served to tourists—my own inner Lynch movie,
complete with a mall and that ice cream for astronauts—

and beneath it all the eye of the blackbird, avian filmmaker
of my interior, paralyzed by its own *Blue Velvet*.

The Future in Half a Pecha Kucha

Making Contact

I've had another letter
from the dinosaurs. They know
what's coming. This time,
they want everything
to be different.

The Future of Cinema

Nights of Cabiria is the only Fellini film
they suggest I take with me.
The dinosaurs love optimism,
especially in Ostian prostitutes
partly scripted by Pasolini.

The Future of Love

People will have sex through straws
pushed together over coke floats
in pharmacies. Love will also
happen through straws.

The Future of Architecture

Buildings will be made
from deconstructive elements.
Their duration will depend
on how long they can
survive under erasure.

The Future of Language

The women words will go to a nunnery,
which will still mean both convent
and whorehouse in Elizabethan slang.
The words for things will no longer pretend
to belong to them, just wander.

The Future of Literary Theory

Criticism will stay the same, impossibly lonely,
classifying bar nuts and buying
shots for nobody before playing
Ace of Base's "The Sign"
on the jukebox.

The Future of Writing

I think they call it graphomania,
the way I'll write curses on everything. These words
will colonize my mind, but I'll be too afraid
to say them. As I dig a pen deeper into my skin,
I'll remember what my father said:
To capture something in words
is an act of violence.

Lies

I wasn't meant for this.
I regularly cut the plastic soda rings
that choke dolphins, play Bingo
with old women, wouldn't set foot
in a brothel.

Truth

I suspect the dinosaurs chose me
because I know how to hang things. I once
made a noose for my Teddy Bear,
punctured his larynx. My only flaw
is that I wasn't meaner to the unicorns.

Saying Goodbye

I wait in a bunker for the dinosaurs
to take me to the future. I've tied
my laces in bows, forgiven
my mother. She was dreaming
and I didn't have the heart
to wake her. I never know why
I cry. It comes on
like a seizure.

A Knowledge of Winged Things

She scares even professionals with her knowledge
of winged things, has stumped
her therapist, an older gentleman

who looks like a mothball. Poor, poor man
of the fanny pack. What does he even keep in there?
Her home has moths. They munch her clothing

when she's not looking, build wingy cities
behind her walls. Sometimes she catches people
looking at her as though she were a strange flying something,

so she understands her pale roommates.
Her friends still marvel at her desire
to live alongside flittering insects. She tells them

You get to a certain age and realize
things aren't so far away from each other after all.
At first she tried to reason with the moths

on the question of eating her clothing.
Let's talk about this like adults, but they kept mum.
She named one, accidentally squished it,

felt terrible, threw it a funeral, and was later haunted by images
of the dead bug's family, by the flurries
of white-winged sorrow she had caused.

If the creature's companions loved it half as much
as she did, they were in for a long evening.
She felt most of all for the moth mother

and her insect version of the human mom's capacity
to fall in love with things left in diapers
like warped Christmas gifts.

A Poem About Poop

I have always wanted to speak of the scatological kingdom
that lives quietly beneath the perfect paint jobs of our lives,
the gritty notes that sound in the hum of any real life,

the gauche, the gross, the truly divine.
Why do we always talk weather?
I want to talk bowel movements,

walk straight up to the next well-bred woman I see,
ask her if she's been regular lately,
whether she works very hard for the lone pellet

or tingles with the fear of what will come
soaring out of her next.
This is what really unites us.

We're not all affected by cold fronts
or the necessity of taking gleaming shovels
to snow, but we all rise in the morning,

trying to guess what our bodies will do,
whether they will obey us or revolt, scattering
pieces of themselves here and there, all the while

pretending that we are neither animal nor savage,
when the unloosed plunk of our private selves
suggests otherwise.

Lunatic Speaks

In the dream I'm under a cow tent
in Africa somewhere, sucking my own sweat
though a straw, feeling that I am nothing

but a sum of small things—snails,
fly wings, dust bunnies, candle drips, leftover air.
When I wake, I feel so empty I eat everything in sight.

My hurt is crystalline,
taking on never-before-seen patterns,
subtle in that way of things

that belong to the mist, like cotton
candy and the blue drool that follows, or the haze
of teeth whiteners and skin powders that leave a dusting

of synthetic snow across the dermis, newly fallen
shadows, so close to not being, spinning
alone in a vacuum.

I still smell of cow and my eyes
have started to rain. I married a weatherman
so that he could tell me when my brain

would start playing "Misty" for me.
The plan backfired and I'm up in the middle of the night
watching TV, can't sleep with this buzzing in my head,

not quite pain and not quite light,
something crueler, a mooing of the mind
trying to run away from itself.

If I'm not crazy, then why do my thoughts
speak a language that I can't understand?
Watching episode after episode of this surgery show

reminds me that people are really just pieces of meat,
tendony, with puffy unindentifiables,
many-colored protrusions

that can be undone with instruments,
like the felling of the first tree
that I do nothing to stop.

3.

Spoon Lover

Food shovel, cradler of air,
tooth mirror, hummingbird toilet,
what are you? Moon-scooper,

rocking horse for pea children,
speak to me. I stare at you until every part
of me becomes an eyeball,

try to see you for the first time,
slice away all sections of brain
that have been touched by spoon,

but then there's nothing. I imagine you
a back-scratcher for ogres,
a silver head on a stick,

a reminder of what becomes of those
who disobey the spoon leader.
Who are you when I'm not around?

Opera lover, birdwatcher, boy scout?
Pervert waiting all day to rub up against
the silvery skin of the other captives

of my silverware drawer? Is that how
the little spoons happen? I stay up
until that hour when taking you

into my mouth becomes inevitable.
As I give up on your grander significance
and eat, I watch you learn what you are.

Astonished by your spoonness,
we learn together. I accept your alien symbols,
your silence. When I suck, you taste metallic,

like cold blood or spoon suicide,
and I see that one night, ravaged
by your own stillness, you'll jump.

In the morning I'll pick your bent body
off the floor, lay you to rest in my mouth, saying,
come unto me, beloved.

Wonderland Therapy

When I first saw you,
curled in toadstool of mind's eye,
I wanted to learn to paint

so I could explain in colors
the conversation of your fur tones,
its shock-talk of hues.

There was pickled awe in my throat
as I looked on you. Even at 7
I knew what you were: *wunderkammer,*

a madness of sense-awakening things,
astonishment soup and wonder mushrooms,
a cabinet of curiosities

much-coveted and positively full of rabbits.
Your hair moves when you move,
as though you were the wind

blowing that hairy planet.
Striped seer, fly me somewhere
on those unfathomable strands.

Your smile is wry on the rocks, Cheshire-style,
a jaunty, crooked marvel, peeking out
of conspicuously unsmiling crowds.

One day I have a wild vision of swimming
in your enormous ears, a fish in waxy waters;
I discover flamingo mallets, the Queen's tarts,

and the Dormouse's dreams.
In this factory of gentleness,
you ease the Hatter's pain,

treat ravens like writing desks,
and go at the endless melancholy
of Mock Turtles with a wrench.

Watching You Suffer

I see you, you know, while you shuffle
around your house, buy coffee
from the street guy, put quarters

in the jukebox after spending
way too long picking your songs.
I'm with you while you draw

fingers through errant hair, raise
a saucy brow, get almost sick with love.
I'm still there after the city halogens go out,

hovering over your explosions
of insomniac thought, curving
in and out of night terrors.

I watch you stay awake after the nightly news,
imagining people being tortured
in suburban basements, crying out

where only metal can hear their
pain ballads, and you almost can't go on,
a shiver building inside you.

On Jury Duty and Motherhood

Who knows why it happened then.
In a Pearl Street courtroom,
seated next to a mouth-breather,

serving my country on a pouring day,
I started thinking about small people crawling out of me,
and by this I mean motherhood.

I am married almost a year now.
My eyes are starting to look
like my grandmother's.

I often wake to find the skin beneath them
creased in bizarre patterns.
I can no longer measure out my life with coffee spoons,

but I've come to need whole crews
of brawny folk with cranes.
My days are the heavy thing

I lug behind me, a stray whale
that followed me home, swimming over concrete
to reach me, love-eyed and soft to the touch.

I saw a camel on TV recently,
and I'm pretty sure we got each other,
we two dromedaries, even-toed ungulates,

wild-eyed creatures of the sand.
I wake some mornings afraid
that I have not grown wise enough,

wishing that I could use my knowledge of earthquakes
to mend my constant need for mourning.
I know that the beginnings of something big are in me

and continue to grow as I breathe, cross streets,
and talk softly to friends in diners—but it's not a baby.
It's a filing cabinet of images, a lens

on a world at once real and imagined.
All of us in that jury room were creatures
locked in a court with our own ghosts,

and I, a fanciful overgrown child,
was thinking about babies.
I can see it in people's eyes.

Married a year? they say
as they size up the situation,
trying to see if I'm fit to flop one out,

as though they have x-ray eyes that can assess
the infrastructure of my inner world of tubes,
the fitness of my baby-making system,

to tell if it's my choice to postpone the arrival
of the small, shriveled person for whom I will be
what I cannot yet be for myself.

Word Pornography

Despite the difference in the smell of the night,
this is our typical post-work evening, you sleep while I type,
but in this after-dark, the sight of your sleeping elbow,

hair-kissed, stroked by the last light of 6:30,
maybe even holy somehow, slays me.
There are so many things I should be doing right now,

but I refuse to stop staring at you. You so often sleep
in long sleeves—it's cruel, really. We women
are insatiable, too, so this peek of meat

makes me both pervert and disciple.
Seeing this unguarded part of you, my mind unfolds
its wonder layers. It's true that I get overwrought too easily,

but who wouldn't covet this unseen slice of you,
this glistening man-thing that lies in my bed
and belongs, miraculously, to me?

I feel lucky on this rainy Thursday to be able to say
that the elbow I have to look at for the rest of my life
is rather ravishing. I write this because, if I don't,

I might run around the neighborhood,
a mad saleswoman hawking your sleepy wares.
I watch you sleep for the marital perk

of seeing pieces of your skin illuminated
by the dying evening light. The green
polka-dotted sheets set your elbow off nicely

and I pay it tribute with my word porn, making you
a centerfold in the magazine of my mind. Right now
I love you so much that I could go fly a kite.

The Truth About Marriage

Hollywood misses the point completely
with its celluloid approximations.
The last shot of the film

where the spray-tanned starlet,
with teeth white as bones picked clean by sea birds,
says "I do" is nothing like it.

Marriage is the place you see
when you close your eyes, the parallel life
you live together in your cave of sheets,

wild-haired, touching softly freckled maps,
raised stretches of scar, your shared land folding
in upon itself in glimmering repose.

It is his unshaven face scrubbing your dry skin
in a pre-toothbrushed morning, mis-aimed man pee,
hairs that grow in places they never should,

the rainbowed chemistry project
at the bottom of your garbage can,
the riotous things toothpaste can do to porcelain,

and that you sometimes still cry
when you fold his clothes
because they've been so close to him.

It is breathing him in the night,
the body surprised at being seen,
the belly not sucked in, muscles unflexed,

private places hanging soft like a long braid.
It is showing him the screaming pieces you usually hide.
Marriage is a man who asks you to be louder.

4.

Planning My Own Funeral

The poetry teacher asked us
how we would like to die.
She meant it as an exercise in absurdity,

but I started thinking seriously
about afterworld investments,
the car I'd like to drive out in.

First I had to figure out
how I wanted to go. I decided
that freezing to nothingness,

asleep in snow, was fitting for a poet,
but it bored me, so instead I decided to die
in a red, screeching, open-backed truck,

hair streaming behind, Tom Waits' *Closing Time*
on the radio. As for the funeral,
let's just be clear, I want bulldogs there.

But before taking to the truck, I have to survive
all the changes that take place in me daily
as I wade through the invisible layers between things.

In addition to pondering death, I've been taking notes on life
that fade away as soon as I mark them down,
like fog-doodled messages on car windows,

trying to solve the riddle of my childhood stage fright.
It wasn't that I didn't want to be seen,
but that I wanted to be seen too much.

The Day I Became a Computer

To whom it may concern,
I leave my human life to you.
As I was writing one morning,

I teetered on the edge of my Mac,
the twinkle of creative failure
looming always like acid soup,

so I put on a mining helmet,
said *screw it* and went in,
stood gaping at that whirring plane

of machine gray matter
that I recognized as my own.
I was halved and the outside air

touching my cyber tissue felt swell,
like the soft pads of a cat
crawling on my electronic kidneys

as I stood, awake in electric sight,
performing a yellow-eyed survey
of the day's outlandish revelations

that brought me still closer to Steve Jobs.
It must have been all those hours
mooning over the hum and glow

of my screen life, that space of literary want,
scrambling over hypertext, tracing link patterns
in pixilated outer space, changing my background image

when in need of a paradigm shift,
emailing with other writers I've never met,
but care about, my inexplicable digital loves.

I blame all those years of waking each morning longing
to commit an act of violence on apathy,
to rip open the aperture of words.

Failing at Fiction

For poetry my fingers storm
computer keys, rush the next
neural connection, my fire lived within.

While I doze, the poem children work.
I wake to a house of exploded lyrics—
all morning they rise.

I go about my day pretending
that I am something more than a poetry factory.
The world loves a good lie, and all the while they rise.

But for fiction my fingers tremble.
Trouble is, the story-child came before the narrative uterus
and now I have nowhere to put it,

so I lug it around behind me
while teaching classes and eating donuts.
Nobody sees it lumbering along

on plot and dialogue yet to be,
a future fiction. The strange and the small
are for me. My mind's motor

runs only in miniature,
seeing not the whole story,
with its allegiance to sense,

but the sensation that fluttered
for a second in the narrator
when he fought the urge to lick a light bulb,

like on New Year's when I couldn't hear the sound
of the crowd, but only the falling confetti pieces
speaking to each other of renewal.

A Poet's Recipe For Working in an Office

First, take about a shopping cart full of nostalgia,
all those snatches of scene, rose-tinged in recollection,
that hover over your days like comic book thought bubbles,

the sometimes symphonic quality of silence,
what it sounds like when indignant people chew lunchmeat,
those minutes stuck in an elevator with the co-worker

who always asks if you're tired, rendered retroactively precious.
Next, mix your ions of productivity with the fever thoughts
that rise up after a night of rugged dreaming,

those snarls of stupor and incubus, of frenzy and ghost story,
of the nightmare you had about the wizards
who moved into your cubicle.

Then stir in all fifty kinds of longing
that battle for the real estate of a single word,
the birds of paradise that are flowers

and the birds-of-paradise that are birds,
and the important questions—like why Garfield was so mean
to Odie, why nobody but Calvin could see Hobbes,

who started the rumor that you like yellow,
and when it would be appropriate to tell your boss
that she's pronouncing your name incorrectly.

Finally, add your reverence for life's margins, those borderlands
where some people stop looking, but you start to see
everything that matters.

Quarterlife Crisis

It has come to this,
startling awake mid-night,
shivery hot and built to spill,

afraid that I will never become
what I should, whatever on earth that is.
Yesterday I saw my face in a window

but she looked nothing like me,
she was not the success story
I made out of feathers as a child.

She was skin and story and visible seams,
but I kind of like seeable scars,
even if every one tells me differently.

Every morning I find articles about younger people
walking on the moon, writing-wise,
while I haven't even mastered Jackson's Moonwalk.

What I am is success seen backwards,
tiny stick sculptures, whisper things.
Structures I want to build with my mind

call out to me from places I can't find
but know better than my own hands
or the smell of my skin in summer.

My desire is that thing I see
while lost in the electronic graveyard
of my computer, when I close my eyes,

a space inside my lids
that looks something like
nighttime on red Mars,

my longing, sweet and scalding,
captured asteroids shaped by a light
that is no more, lunatic and lavender,

some spiritual world gone topsy-turvy,
a planet spinning out of control,
half a cat smile, a fallen winged thing.

The Day She Lost Her Love

Every day she wakes without a tongue,
but she speaks all the time
to the one she lost.

Where she visits him
there are stars everywhere,
self-luminous bodies on the streets,

children throwing twinkling balls of gas in the park,
the clunk of angels finally getting their flying gear.
Somewhere along the way a pause descended,

and she realized in matters of life and death
there is more than the before and the beyond.
Because the motion of their days

had been rings of fingerprint logic,
they spun together in circles till he faded.
Sometimes she remembers their living world—

his climbing the ladder of her messy curls
in the morning, a slight smell of the breakfast
he made them on his fingers,

the tenderness of a life together.
Then later came the ache
of untouched food and emptied eyes,

but her final words weren't "I love you"
because he wouldn't have liked that.
Instead, she said, *I stayed*

to hear you tell the same story
that everyone else had told me,
only when you told it, I laughed.

All About My Mother

There I am thinking in two directions at once,
trying to find the glasses on my head, spewing mind juice
all over my papers. Yet there must be some grace
to this unbecoming mambo because I do it daily
in the gleam of the kitchen's luminous eye.

The lamp, a synthetic seasonal happiness
shining down on my working head, reveals what I hide.
I'll be 27 soon and have started finding white hairs—
not just strays, but whole colonies of snow fur.
I pull them out, bashfully at first, and then with startling
      violence.

These hairs crouch together in a field of brown,
white buildings sprung from the architecture
of my years. They have even spawned a kind of language
to converse with the other hair creatures. I know this
because at night I hear them chattering.

My mom's hair is white-blonde. There she is,
throwing popcorn to the dog again. This is their game:
the Airedale lives for it, trundling her blonde behind
like a truck backing up to receive the salty treats.

My mother responds with her part of the act,
raining popped kernels down upon the jolly beast.
You're wackadoodle, I tell her, and she smiles toothily.
In this moment, time's wormhole has made a space for us
and I understand her. I reach over, take her hand, squeeze,
and then together we throw the glowing corn.

Acknowledgments

This book owes so much to my friends, family, and teachers who helped me along the way. Thanks to Marty Skoble, Elisabeth Frost, Heather Dubrow, Jennifer Ryan, Danita Geltner, Dorinda Wegener, Julie Tetel, Veronica Russo, Barish Ali, Peter Ramos, Karen Sands-O'Connor, Mitch Levenberg, Charley Gerard, Judi Weinstock, Eva Gerard, Trish and Louis Hagood, Erica Wright, Nicholas and Meg Birns, Miku Terai, Julie Mulligan, Daniella Furman, Barb Williams, Linda Greenberg, Diane Kistner, and Adriel Gerard.

Many thanks to the journals in which the following poems first appeared:

Huffington Post: "The Day I Became a Computer"
Into the Teeth of the Wind: "All About My Mother"
kill author: "My Inner David Lynch Movie," "Gender Studies,"
    "A Knowledge of Winged Things"
Manhattan Chronicles: "Word Pornography"
Mouse Tales Press: "Lunatic Speaks"
Poetic Matrix: "What Lolita Wishes She Could Say"
Quail Bell Magazine: "Word Painting of a Psychiatrist"
    (an earlier version of "Wonderland Therapy")
Radius: "Watching You Suffer"
RootSpeak: "Quarterlife Crisis"

*Cover art, "Fuji Butterfly (inversion)," by Dominic Alves
(flickr.com/photos/dominicspics); cover and book design
by Diane Kistner (dkistner@futurecycle.org)*

About FutureCycle Press

FutureCycle Press is dedicated to publishing lasting English-language poetry and flash fiction books, chapbooks, and anthologies in both print-on-demand and ebook formats. Founded in 2007 by long-time independent editor/publishers and partners Diane Kistner and Robert S. King, the press incorporated as a nonprofit in 2012. A number of our editors are distinguished poets and authors in their own right, and we have been actively involved in the small press movement going back to the early seventies.

Our annual anthology, *FutureCycle*, combines poetry and flash fiction. The FutureCycle Poetry Book Prize and honorarium is awarded annually for the best full-length volume of poetry we publish in a calendar year. We are dedicated to giving all authors we publish the care their work deserves, making our catalog of titles the most distinguished it can be, and paying forward any earnings to fund more great books.

We've learned a few things about independent publishing over the years. We've also evolved a unique, resilient publishing model that allows us to focus mainly on vetting and preserving for posterity the most books of exceptional quality without becoming overwhelmed with bookkeeping and mailing, fundraising activities, or taxing editorial and production "bubbles." To find out more about what we are doing, come see us at www.futurecycle.org.